IRISH
PROVERBS

IRISH
PROVERBS

Compiled by the Editors of Hippocrene Books

ILLUSTRATED BY
Fergus Lyons

HIPPOCRENE BOOKS
New York

For information, address:
HIPPOCRENE BOOKS, INC.
171 Madison Avenue
New York, NY 10016

ISBN 0-7818-0676-3

Design and composition by Susan Ahlquist, Perfect Setting.

Cataloging-in-Publication Data available from the Library of Congress.

Printed in the United States of America.

*This book is dedicated to the memory of
Eugene F. Williams.*

Irish Proverbs

Young people don't know what age is,
and old people
forget what youth was.

The angels know each other.

The thing that often occurs is
never much appreciated.

A dimple in the chin, a devil within.

The "bad drop" runs in a family
for seventeen generations.

It is a hard fought battle from which no man
returns to tell the tale.

There's no crime in the blow that
has not been struck.

The devil never grants long leases.

If you go to the court, leave your soul at home.

A full cabin is better than an empty castle.

Don't lift me till I fall.

Seeing is believing, but feeling is God's own truth.

Three feasts due to everyone: the feast of baptism,
of marriage, and of death.

It is the children of the fortunate who make the unfortunate people.

There is no strength without unity.

He who steals the fire steals the blessing.

Eaten bread is soon forgotten.

Let broth boil slowly, let porridge make a noise.

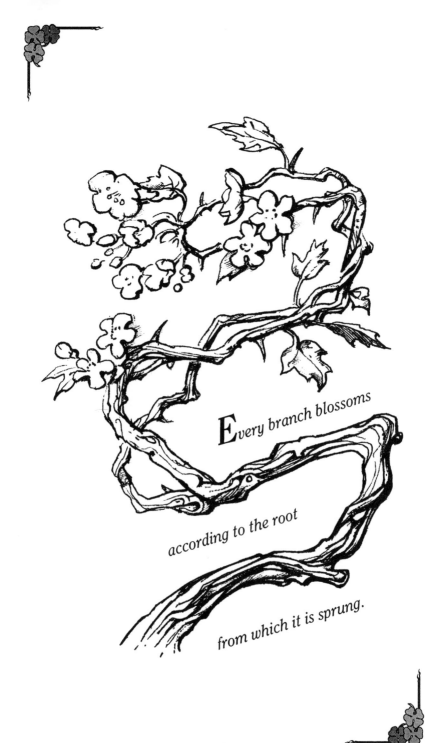

Every branch blossoms

according to the root

from which it is sprung.

Grass and carelessness.
(This is said to be the best method for rearing young cattle
as too much attention does more harm than good.)

He who is nearest to church is last
walking up to Mass.

Clean and whole make poor clothes shine.

She burnt the coal and did not warm herself.

W̲hat is there that seems worse to a man than his death, and yet he does not know but it may be the height of his good luck.

'T̲is for the sake of the company the dogs go to church.

E̲ight views, eight recollections.

T̲here is often the death of a person between two words.

There are white flowers on the fisherman's garden.
(Said when the sea is white with breakers.)

The strong man when he wants to;
the weak man when he's able.

Don't give cherries to pigs,
don't give advice to fools.

There are two things that cannot be cured:
death and the want of sense.

A Kerry shower is of twenty-four hours.

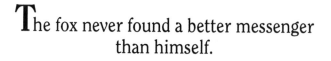

The fox never found a better messenger
than himself.

God's help is nearer than the door.

It is well that misfortune comes but from time to
time and not all together.

Though honey is sweet, do not lick it off a briar.

*You'll never plough a field
by turning it over in your mind.*

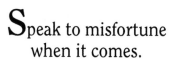

Speak to misfortune
when it comes.

Love conceals, hate sees
a multitude of faults.

Even contention is better than loneliness.

Woe to him who does not heed
a good wife's counsel.

A man never falls among his own people.

Poor men take to the sea,
rich men to the mountain.

A person and his appearance
often contradict each other.

Wisdom does not come
before age.

Better good manners than good looks.

Trust not a spiteful man.

A foot at rest means nothing.

The fox never sent out a messenger
better than himself.

The effects of an evil act are long felt.

Woe to him whose betrayer sits at his table.

Be on your guard against taking sides and on no account sacrifice your friends.

Choose your company before you sit down.

Slow is every foot on an unknown path.

A wise man makes a closed mouth.

The mouth that speaks not,

is sweet to hear.

Tell me with whom thou goest and
I'll tell thee what thou doest.

Say but little and say it well.

Shallow waters make a great noise.

Evening is speedier than morning.

Want is a good guide.

A late man brings trouble onto himself.

Don't make little of your dish for it may be an ignorant fellow who judges it.

The evening is a good prophet.

When you have a desire to do anything your feet are light.

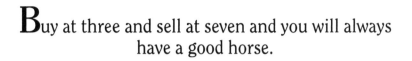

Buy at three and sell at seven and you will always
have a good horse.

A misty winter, a frosty spring, a varied summer,
and a sunny harvest is an ideal year.

Love all men barring an attorney.

Pity him who makes an opinion a certainty.

Live in my heart and pay no rent.

Its better to be lucky than to be an early riser.

Marry in haste and be sorry in your leisure.

What occurs but once will be forgotten forever.

It's a lonely wash that has no man's shirt in it.

Stupidity is sending the goose on a message to the fox's den.

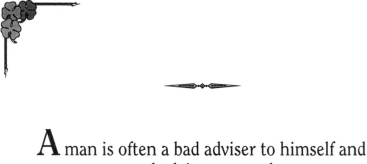

A man is often a bad adviser to himself and
a good adviser to another.

He might die of wind but he'll never die of wisdom.

Time is a good storyteller.

Fortune comes in a slender stream,
but misfortune in a torrent.

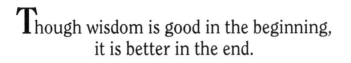

Though wisdom is good in the beginning,
it is better in the end.

Everything troubles you and the cat
breaks your heart.

Love lives a short while, but hate lives for long.

That which is not eaten or stolen will be found.

Your son is your son today, but your daughter is your daughter forever.

Both your friend and your enemy think you'll never die.

What I am afraid to hear, I'd better say first myself.

If you wish to be reviled, marry; if you wish to be praised, die.

Nature breaks
through the eyes of the cat.

27

A friend's eye is a good mirror.

The man who won't take advice will have conflict.

'Tis the hope of satisfaction that ruins the gambler.

Even a small thorn can cause festering.

A wise man takes advice.

The well-filled belly has little understanding of the empty.

You never had neighbors as good as boundary fences.

"Often" is not honored.

Peace is worth purchasing.

The solution to every question is found in itself.

What is seldom is tasty.

Let him cool in the skin he heated in.

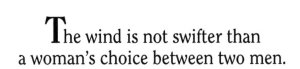

The wind is not swifter than
a woman's choice between two men.

Give your love to your wife and
your secret to your mother.

Every man's mind is his kingdom.

There are fish in the sea,
better than have ever been caught.

Two shorten the road.

Take gifts with a sigh, most men give to be paid.

A whisper in Nora's ear is louder than
a shout from the highest hill.

The herb that can't be got is the one that
brings relief.

The beginning of a ship is a board, of a kiln a stone,
of a King's reign salutation and
the beginning of health is sleep.

What butter or whiskey will not cure,
there is no cure for.

A patch is better than a hole but a hole is
more honorable than a patch.

It is more difficult to maintain honor
than to become prosperous.

Go to a man in difficulty and you will get yourself
a bargain.

There has not been found, nor will there be found, a juster judge than the field of battle.

A constant beggar gets a constant refusal.

A man may live after losing his life but not after losing his honor.

Good is never late.

He that loves danger shall perish in it.

Be afraid and you'll be safe.

Four things Irishman ought not trust: a cow's horn,
a horse's hoof, a dog's snarl and
an Englishman's laugh.

When the belly is full the bones like to stretch.

That which is rare is wonderful.

In the world of the blind the one-eyed man is king.

There is no crime in the blow that
has not been struck.

In youth we have our troubles before us,
in age we have our pleasures behind us.

Drunkenness and anger, it is said, speaks truly.

Nobility listens to art.

A mouth of ivy and a heart of holly.

By their tongues people are caught,
by their horns, cattle.

He who is bad at giving a lodging
is good at showing the road.

The law of borrowing is
to break the borrower.

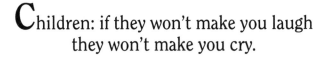

Children: if they won't make you laugh
they won't make you cry.

Every finger has not the same length,
nor every son the same disposition.

Be one's trade good or bad, it is experience
that makes one adept at it.

Falsehood often goes further than truth.

---◆---

The proof of the pudding lies in the eating of it.

---◆---

Pity the man who is drowned during the tempest,
for after the rain comes the sun.

---◆---

A soft answer may turneth away wrath.

---◆---

Love
pursuits
profit.

---◆---

The mountain is good mustard
(hunger is the best sauce).

Praise the ripe field not the green corn.

Truth may be bitter.

Let not your tongue cut your throat.

A shut fist gets only a closed hand.

Fame endures longer than life.

Time and tide wait for no man.

Better one good thing that is than
two good things that were.

Patience is a plaster for all sores.

The fear of God is the beginning of wisdom.

One look before is better than two behind.

Rent to a lord is like food to a child.

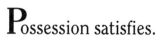

 S leep is a brother to death.

 T wo-thirds of sickness belong to the night,
two-thirds of folly belong to the youth,
two-thirds of covetousness belong to the old,
two-thirds of talk belong to the drinking folk.

 N o war is more bitter than the war of friends,
but it does not last long.

 P ossession satisfies.

Burning embers are easily kindled.

Marry a mountainy woman and you'll marry the whole mountain.

Speed and precision do not agree.

To a man equipped for war, peace is answered.

What the child sees the child does.

There is no welcome for one who borrows.

Eaten bread is soon forgotten.

The three merriest things:
a cat's kitten, a goat's kid and a young widow.

Money swore an oath that nobody that did not
love it should ever have it.

No feast is without a roast piece;
no real torment is experienced until marriage.

Bend with the tree that
bends with you.

There's
no tax
on talk.

Every man's mind is his kingdom.

Death stares the old in the face
and lurks behind
the back of the young.

Greatness knows modesty.

Though I have
the books
I don't have
the learning.

Don't show your skin to the person
who won't cover it.

A little help is better than
a deal of pity.

Woe to him who is not content with
having God for his sustenance.

There is often a barb behind a kiss.

A sweet tongue is seldom without
a sting to its root.

No two people ever lit a fire
without disagreeing.

Desire conquers fear.

He would go to Mass every morning
if holy water were whiskey.

Time
is a good
storyteller.

Wine revels in truth.

A trade not learned is an enemy.

Truth is bitter, but never shamed.

The cure of the drinking is to drink again.

The old pipe gives
the sweetest smoke.

A scholar's ink lasts longer than a martyr's blood.

———◆———

What should you expect from a cat but a kitten.

———◆———

There is no anguish of soul until one has children.

———◆———

The closed hand gets the shut fist.

———◆———

Fate is stronger than rearing.

———◆———

Take gifts with a sigh, most men give to be paid.

If you go to a feast uninvited, bring your own stool.

Good luck beats early rising.

The blackest thorn bears the whitest blossom.

If you don't get the meat, the soup is worth a lot.

The longest road out is the shortest road home.

The person bringing good news
knocks boldly on the door.

Three things that pertain to age:
greed, hair, and fingernails.

Forgetting a debt
doesn't mean
it's paid.

A combed head sells the feet.

Comfort is not known if poverty does not
come before it.

Two-thirds of help is to give courage.

There was never great love that was not followed
by great hate.

If it's drowning you're after,
don't torment yourself
with shallow water.

A constant guest is never welcome.

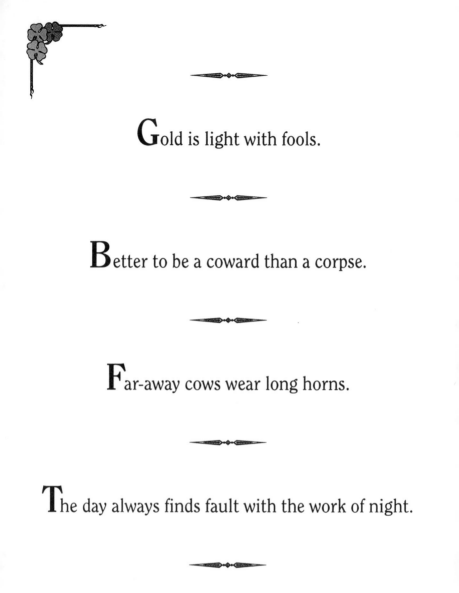

Gold is light with fools.

Better to be a coward than a corpse.

Far-away cows wear long horns.

The day always finds fault with the work of night.

Life is a strange lad.

One pair of good soles is worth
two pairs of uppers.

Keep your shop and your shop will keep you.

The fox is never deceived twice.

A person's tongue often cuts his throat.

Health is better than herds of cattle.

Thirst and the love disease know no shame,
but the itch leaves them hollow.

It's no secret that is known to three.

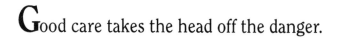

Good care takes the head off the danger.

Sleepiness is the sign of death in a man and
watchfulness in a woman.

Seldom is the last of anything better than the first.

'Tis hard to escape the bonds of love.

Death is the poor man's best physician.

Listen to the river and you will catch a trout.

———⊶◆⊷———

A good denial is the best point in law.

———⊶◆⊷———

He who has lived a long life has many a story.

———⊶◆⊷———

I have but little, and that is wholesome for myself.

We live as long as we're let.

Better a lock than doubt.
(i.e. security)

Loneliness is better than bad company.

An Irishman often breaks his nose with his mouth.

The river is no wider
from this side
than the other.

Blow not on dead embers.

Love veils
the unlovely.

Aristotle could not divine what
an autumn night would do.

A woman's first love, a man's second,
these endure most.

What is got badly
goes badly.

Hope protects the oppressed.

A kind word never broke
anyone's mouth.

A person often ties a knot with his tongue
that his teeth cannot untie.

Questioning is the door of knowledge.

Never give the devil good-morrow
till you meet him.

The poor man's cow and the rich man's son
are two things that will die.

A dimple in the chin,
a devil within.

Never bolt your door with a boiled carrot.

Where there is dowry
there is danger.

As wet as drammock.
(Drammock is raw oatmeal and water.)

If the cat had a dowry, it's often her mouth
would be kissed.

Love's a disease that no herb cures.

Take the drink for the thirst that is yet to come.

Better to be an old man's pet than
a young man's slave.

A narrow neck keeps the bottle from being emptied
in one swill.

Men are like bagpipes,
no sound comes from them
till they're full.

79

Don't desert the highway for the shortcut.

Hope is the physician of each misery.

The devil makes work for idle hands.

The body would like well to leave fasting to the soul.

An art is better than a heritage.

Fear is worse than fighting.

Don't lift me till I fall.

The people go but the hills remain.

Good care never yet destroyed anything.

A sore heart makes a feeling one.

Better is an ass that carries you than a horse
that throws you.

A drink of the door.
(i.e. a parting drink)

Evening is speedier than morning.

I don't cook my cabbage twice.
(Said when a person is asked to repeat a remark or tale.)

The biggest help
is help and
even the smallest help is help.

Do not turn your back on anything but on
going to hell.

A new broom sweeps clean, but the old brush
knows the corners.

Grief has no cure but to kill it with patience.

Happiness follows simplicity.

When your haste is greatest your delay is greatest.

Unwillingness easily finds an excuse.

A man never fails among his own people.

*A*fter a gathering

comes a scattering.

All good has an end save the goodness of God.

If you want to advertise a thing,
tell it to a woman as a secret.

Who gossips with you will gossip of you.

Wisdom is often hard.

Greatness knows gentleness.

It is sweet to drink but bitter to pay for.

When the drop is inside the sense is outside.

The well fed do not understand the lean.

Do not put the ease before the hardship.

A person's heart is
in his feet.

Between poverty and riches there is but one year.

Wine divulges truth.

No one knows which is best, early or late.

Better to have a cloak on your shoulder than to have the doctor's horse at your door.

He who has water and peat on his own farm has the world his own way.

It is better to be in search of food than of appetite.

Prosperity on your hand, and may God
always leave the stretch in it.
(i.e. may you always have something to give)

One must pay health its tithe.

The three kinds of people who will quickest
get to heaven after their death:
a young child after baptism,
a young priest after ordination,
and the poor tiller of the soil.

No one ever went to hell
without sixpence
at the time of his death.
(A relic of pagan burial custom.)

A storm does not go beyond Sunday,
nor a spring-tide beyond Wednesday.

What would the cat's son do,
but kill a mouse.

The eleventh commandment:
look after yourself.

Never sell a hen on a wet day.

As idle as a piper's little finger.

It's as slippery as an eel's belly.

Promise much and there will be many
in search of you.

A slow hound is often happy.

Though the day be long, night will come.

Many a ragged colt made a noble horse.

It is not natural to have smoke without fire
nor fire without people.

Two days in the spring are as good as
ten days in harvest.

The stars make
no noise.

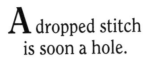

A dropped stitch
is soon a hole.

B oil a stone in butter and its juice will be drunk.

H owever long you remain away from home, don't
bring home a bad story about yourself.

B etter strife
than solitude.

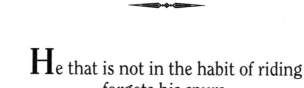

He that is not in the habit of riding
forgets his spurs.

———◆———

Who brings a tale
takes two away.

———◆———

Whoever may be king,
tea is queen.

———◆———

Tears bring nobody back
from the grave.

———◆———

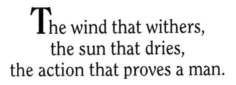

The wind that withers,
the sun that dries,
the action that proves a man.

Three things that cannot be taught: a singing voice,
generosity, and poetry.

Often was ugly amiable and
handsome unfortunate.

All wealth is consumed by small spending.

It's no use carrying an umbrella if your shoes are leaking.

Three men fail to understand women: young men, old men and middle-aged men.

If you want to know what God thinks of money just look at who he gives it to.

A ship has often sunk close to the harbor.

For a deed which cannot be undone, patience is best.

There is no wind in the air that is not
in somebody's sails.

Put silk on a goat and it is still a goat.

A little blood-relationship is better than a lot
of friendship.

He who is not strong
needs to be clever.

The calf belongs to the man who owns the cow.

He who has most books is not the one who has most learning.

If you lose an hour in the morning, you'll be looking for it all day.

The vengeance of God is direct, even if it is slow.

The good thing that is,
is better than
the two good things
that were.

There is no strength
until there is
cooperation.

If you sow undersized potatoes,
you will harvest
undersized potatoes.

The young crab has the same walk as the old crab.

The wheel which is turning doesn't rust.

Grass doesn't grow on a busy road.

Much wants more.

Better to rule Hell thank to serve in Heaven.

It's a long road that has no bend.

Those the gods can't lead they will drag.

Other Irish interest titles from Hippocrene. . .

Irish Love Poems: DÁNTA GRÁ
edited by Paula Redes
Illustrated by Peadar McDaid

Mingling the famous, the infamous, and the unknown into a striking collection, these works span four centuries up to the most modern of poets such as Nuala Ní Dhomhnaill and Brendan Kennelly.

146 pages • 6 X 9 • illus. • 0-7818-0396-9 • W • $17.50hc • (70)

Treasury of Irish Love Poems, Proverbs & Triads
edited by Gabriel Rosenstock

This compilation of over 70 Irish love poems, proverbs and triads spans 15 centuries and features original works and English translations of poetry from such prominent Irish poets as Colm Breathnach and Nuala Ní Dhomhnaill. With selections exploring the realm of lost love, first love, and love's powerful grasp, discover why this book is essential to any Irish literature collection—and discover why "The power of poetry, coupled with the power of love, is alive and well and living in Ireland."

153 pages • 5 X 7 • 0-7818-0644-5 • W • $11.95hc • (732)

Ogham: An Irish Alphabet
Críostóir Mag Fhearaigh
Illustrated by Tim Stampton

The form of Irish known as Ogham was established as a medium of written communication by the fourth century A.D. Ogham is believed to have been influenced by the Latin alphabet and consists of twenty letters each represented by one or more lines or notches carved along a vertical line, for example along the edge of a standing stone, as illustrated in this book. *Ogham: An Irish Alphabet* is a bilingual explanation and an illustrated representation of the ancient and enigmatic Ogham alphabet.

80 pages • 5 ½ X 8 ½ • 0-7818-0665-8 • $7.95pb • (757)

Irish Grammar: A Basic Handbook

Noel McGonagle

Students who are beginners, adults who need to brush up, or teachers in need of a trustworthy reference guide will welcome this handy, straightforward grammar handbook with its attractive format and easy-to-use approach. Noel McGonagle is a lecturer in the Modern Irish Department in University College, Galway. He has written extensively on linguistic and literary aspects of Modern Irish.

100 pages • 5 ¼ X 7 ½ • 0-7818-0667-4 • NA • $9.95pb • (759)

Irish-English/English-Irish Dictionary and Phrasebook

This 1,400-word dictionary indicates pronunciation in English spelling and will swiftly acquaint visitors with a basic key vocabulary. Phrases cover travel, sightseeing, shopping, and recreation, and notes are provided on grammar, pronunciation, and dialect.

171 pages • 3 ¾ X 7 • 1,400 entries/phrases • 0-87052-110-1 • NA • $7.95pb • (385)

Prices subject to change without notice. **To purchase Hippocrene Books** contact your local bookstore, call (718) 454-2366, or write to: HIPPOCRENE BOOKS, 171 Madison Avenue, New York, NY 10016. Please enclose check or money order, adding $5.00 shipping (UPS) for the first book and $.50 for each additional book.